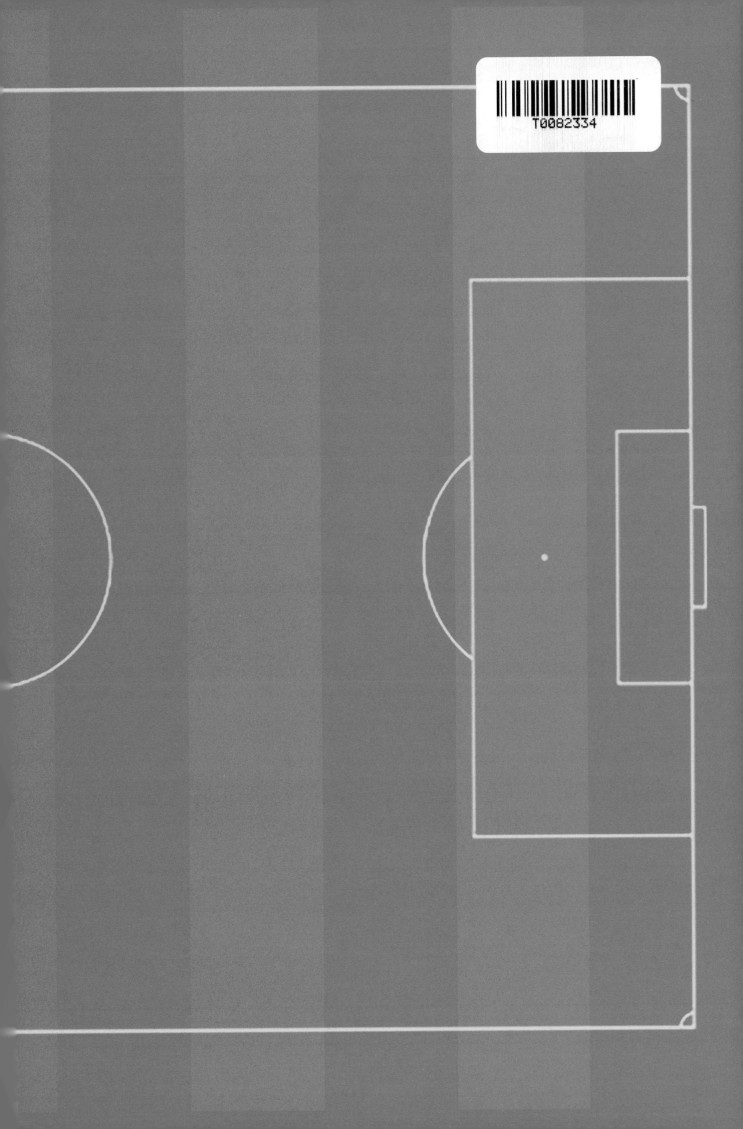

So
Que

poems

Charles R. Smith Jr.

CANDLEWICK PRESS

Contents

"Go Ahead, Abby": A Soccer Chant

Go ahead, Abby,
lead the way
lead the way.
Use your head, Abby,
that's the way
that's the way,
score a goal
for the USA!

Hey hey hey!

Go ahead, Abby,
lead the chase
lead the chase.
Use your foot, Abby,
that's the way
that's the way,
score a goal
for the USA!

Hey hey hey!

Make your mark, Abby,
with your play
with your play.
No one's tougher than you
when you play
when you play,
score a goal
for the USA!

Hey hey hey!

That's our Abby
we're proud to say,
you're a champion
A CHAMPION
in every way,
you led the way
for the USA!

Abby Wambach

Automatic

Fútbol fans,
  clap your hands
  stomp your feet in the stands
  then turn your attention
  onto the pitch
  to witness the magic
  of **Automatic Alex** . . .

The **Goal Hunter**
on a scoring mission,
sprinting
spinning
weaving
as the **Toe Tactician**,
disappearing behind defenders
reappearing as the **Magician**,
finishing with diabolical
between-the-leg kick-ins.

  Lethal Weapon
  launching long-range rockets,
  lobbing overhead
  into-the-net goalie shockers.

The Airbender,
around-the-shoulder sender,
penalty-kick-punching
game-winning
dream ender,
punching holes
into the goal
left
right
and
center.
Jump-hugging teammate
tea-sipping celebrator,
Automatic Alex
MESMERIZING spectators!

Alex Morgan

The Prote

Acrobatic

leaping

slapping

trapping

fearless

relentless

Briana

saving

Briana Scurry

ctors

Athletic

diving

cat-quick

sliding

confident

amazing

Alyssa

saving

Alyssa Naeher

Lightning

Ominous
clouds
erase the blue sky
as cleats
churn
and burn
and fly,
going fast
fast
fast
fast,
crackling the air
rumbling the grass.

Sparks from the goal
attract heat
from feet,
clicking
sizzling
sparking
cleats.
Thunder
EXPLODES
when sparks connect
as **Lightning Lloyd**
SCORCHES the net.

Carli Lloyd

The Express

Speed and finesse,
the Express
Christen Press,
on the move
on the run
sending shots
into nets.
Kicking
and chasing
and pushing
the pace in
the middle
zig-zagging
and sprinting
and racing,

turning
then flipping
then catching
then trapping,
then flicking
the ball
up
then tapping
right toe
to left toe
to right knee
to chest
to right instep
chipping
the ball in a crest
over the goalie
billowing the nets,
another goal delivered
by **the Express!**

Christen Press

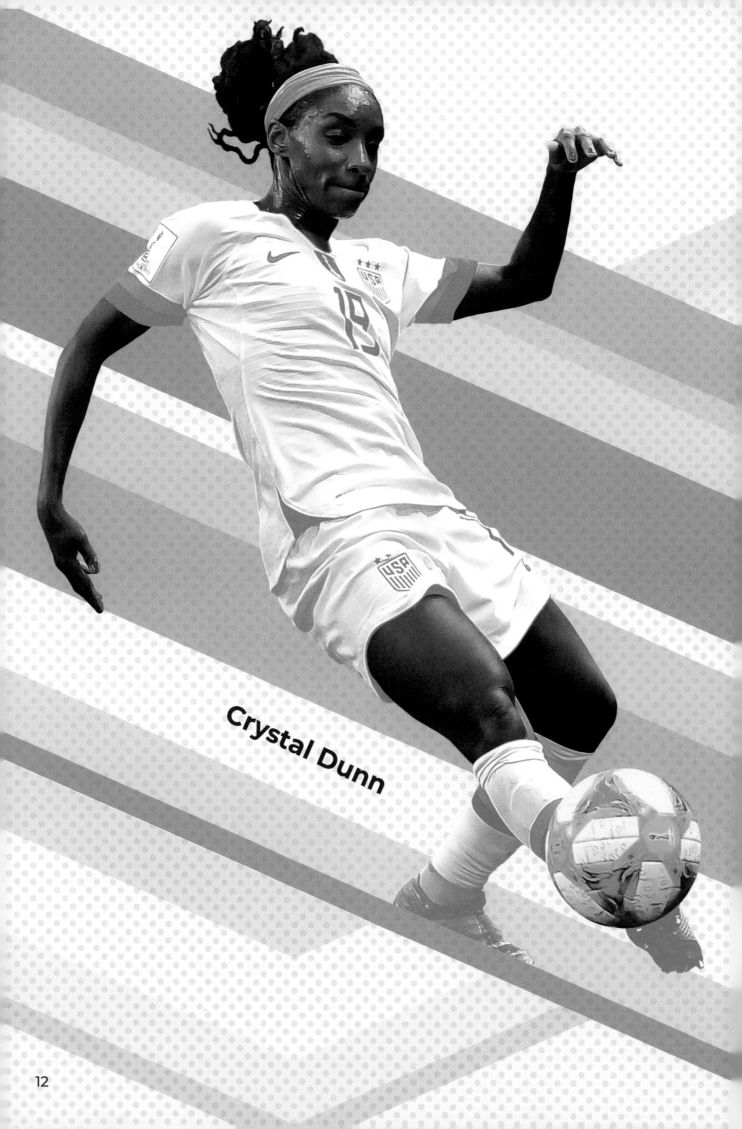

Crystal Dunn

Dunn and Done

		done
Clutch		done
Right foot		done
		done
utilit**Y**		done
Speed		done
Tackles		done
Assists		
Left foot		

Crystal Dunn **gets it done.**

The Wall

Julie Ertz

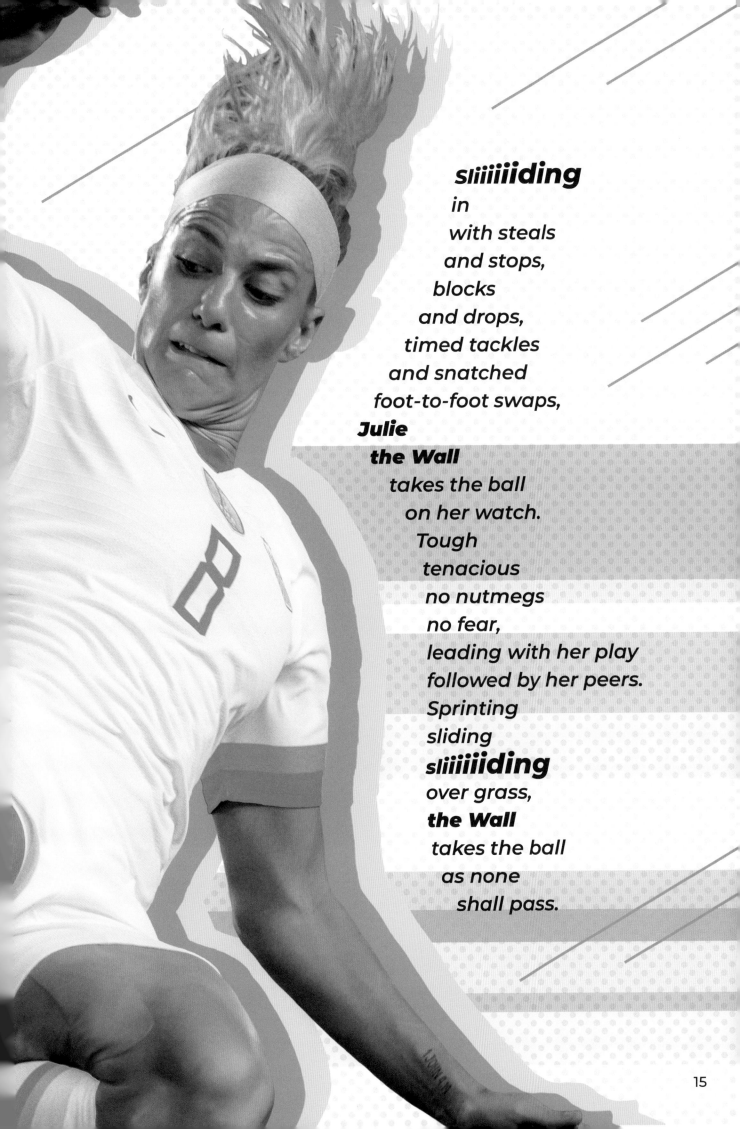

sliiiiiiding
in
with steals
and stops,
blocks
and drops,
timed tackles
and snatched
foot-to-foot swaps,
Julie
the Wall
takes the ball
on her watch.
Tough
tenacious
no nutmegs
no fear,
leading with her play
followed by her peers.
Sprinting
sliding
sliiiiiiding
over grass,
the Wall
takes the ball
as none
shall pass.

15

Kelley O'Hara

A Limerick for Kelley O'Hara

On the pitch **Kelley O'Hara** did play,

tackling and **taking** the ball away,

then racing **downfield**

before kicking **midfield**

for a **teammate to score** on the play!

Rocket Rapinoe

10 toes thrust
ball across grass

9 yards from goal

8 players propelled past

7 strides separate

6 feet racing

5 steps spin

4 bodies chasing

3 breaths

2 eyes
lock on target

1 leg launches
a goal-scoring
rocket!

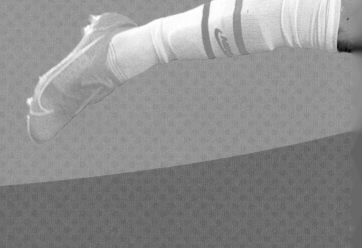

Megan Rapinoe

The Escape Artist

Here she comes
here she comes
on the run
on the run,
the Escape Artist Rose
eluding everyone.
One defender
two defenders
three form a wall
but with a **stop**
go
scoop
Rose **escapes** with the ball.
Toe kick
heel touch
feet push with pace
accelerating away
from legs giving chase,
then **four defenders** circle
Rose.
Can she escape?

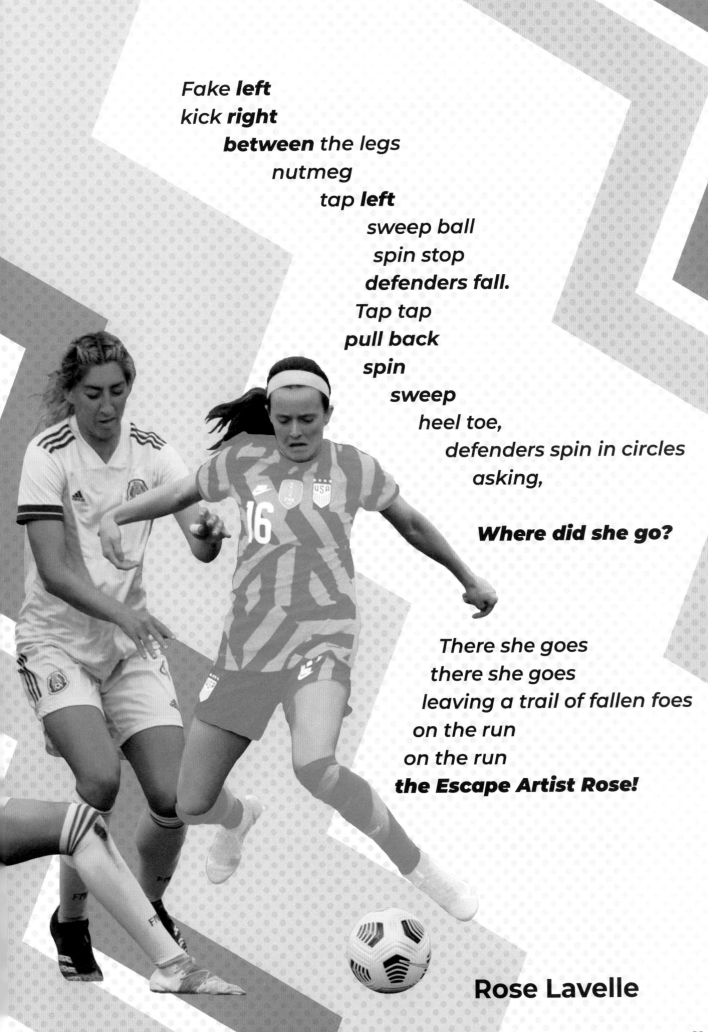

Fake **left**
kick **right**
   between the legs
      nutmeg
      tap **left**
         sweep ball
         spin stop
         defenders fall.
      Tap tap
      pull back
      spin
         sweep
            heel toe,
               defenders spin in circles
               asking,

   Where did she go?

      There she goes
      there she goes
      leaving a trail of fallen foes
      on the run
      on the run
      the Escape Artist Rose!

Rose Lavelle

17

Tobin Heath

Tobin *walking*.
Tobin *stalking*.
Tobin *stepping*.
Tobin *jogging*.
Tobin *sprinting*.
Tobin *stopping*.
Tobin *starting*.
Tobin *chopping*.
Tobin *dragging*.
Tobin *flicking*.
Tobin *spinning*.
Tobin *tricking*.
Tobin *splitting*.
Tobin *faking*.
Tobin *taking*.
Tobin *making*.

Mia Hamm

Motivation In Action

'99ers

With the crest
on their chest
representing
the US,
twenty women
scratch
athletes
scratch
ballers
came to test
their skills against the world
to find out who's the best.
Led by captain Carla
on a **World Cup quest**,
the squad,
from game one,
came to play
and impressed.

First goal on the board
brought the crowd to a **roar**
when the left foot of Mia
launched a rocket to score.
Two more would follow
from Foudy and Lilly,
giving the Americans
their first victory.

Game two
game three
two more victories
with nine goals scored
by multiple feet:
Hamm, Milbrett, Akers, Lilly,
Parlow, MacMillan,
and Venturini.
Game four
their biggest test
against Germany
when Chastain kicked an
      own goal
and got down early.
But Milbrett scored
to tie the game,
then Germany scored,
then a goal by Chastain
tied it again,
until Fawcett came through
with a goal for the **win**.

Next up, Brazil
in the semifinal,
facing top scorer, Sissi,
to get to the final.
Brazil came out
taking shot
after shot
but Briana blocked them all
until the clock **stopped**.
A penalty kick from Akers,
an early goal from Parlow
advanced the Americans
to the World Cup final.

USA versus China
in the Rose Bowl,
the energy **electric**
to see the first goal.
A rematch of the Olympics
three years before
in the gold medal game,
ended with no score.
So penalty kicks
would determine victory,
the first time ever
in women's World Cup
history.

China went first
then the USA,
each taking their shot
from just twelve yards away.
First player
second player
scored on each side
but China's third player
Briana **denied**
with a dive to the left side
firing up the crowd,
loud and **wide-eyed**.
3 kicks for China
2 goals on the board
put China behind
when Lilly scored
then China
then Mia
then China again,

leaving one kick
on the foot of Chastain,
leaving one kick
to decide the game.
One kick
left foot
to the right side,
back of the net **GOAL**
fist pump to the sky.
Shirt off
knee drop
Chastain is **snapped,**
as the world watches
and the crowd claps.
The team celebrates
their World Cup victory,
the team that emphasized
"we" over "me,"
the team that connected
as one family
inspired a generation
of girls to compete,
the **'99ers**
kicked
their name into history.

POEM NOTES

I played plenty of sports when I was younger, but soccer wasn't one of them. Sure, I could kick a ball around, but I never played in games and didn't know the rules or positions. But in 2019, like everyone else, I got caught up in the excitement of watching the US Women's National Team in the World Cup. The game was fast, the players were skilled, and the competition was fierce. But there were the Americans, beating opponents and making it look easy. Ultimately, they defended their crown, won four years earlier, and built a solid foundation to continue their dominance for years to come.

It wasn't always this way. It wasn't until the '99ers broke through and showed everyone that not only could the ladies win but crowds would support them. That's why they're featured here with the story of their 1999 World Cup chase from start to finish. Players from that squad inspired many of today's stars, who now inspire future stars.

When it came to writing about the players, I got a chance to focus on what made each of them stand out. But since I didn't play soccer, I had to learn the rules and the positions of the game. This introduced me to specific words used in soccer, which, like each sport, has its own terminology. I used that information to lock in on the most exciting players at each position. Then I watched videos—lots and lots and lots of videos—to study each player and find something unique about them. There are players from different eras, and I had the freedom to just write. But first, I had to figure out whom to include.

Mia Hamm was the first player I wrote about because she's Mia Hamm, the first woman to put a face on women's soccer. She was extremely skilled at scoring goals and played with a ferocity that caught the world's eye. I love the simplicity of her name and the fact that her first name alone is so recognizable. I used those three simple letters in an acrostic to show what she's all about.

The next player I wrote about was Abby Wambach. Watching games played all over the world, I saw how the fans chanted in the stands. I also noticed that Abby seemed to shine brightest in the biggest games. So I created a chant for her that I could imagine fans shouting as she played.

Megan Rapinoe gets so much attention off the field, I knew I would write about her. After watching a few videos of Megan, I said to myself, *She has a rocket in her leg*, and Rocket Rapinoe was born. Rockets always have a countdown before they take off, so I ended the poem with the rocket launching into the goal.

While learning about the game, I noticed that many of the players played multiple positions, so I tried to mention that while focusing on what they did best. For Julie Ertz, it was her sliding tackles. For Crystal Dunn, it was her do-anything-needed game. For Kelley O'Hara, it was her assists, and since she is of Irish heritage, I wrote her poem as a limerick.

Then there were the dribblers. They were the most fun to write about because it was like watching poetry in motion. Seeing Rose Lavelle escape defender after defender, I gave her the title the Escape Artist. Tobin Heath used her dribbling in a different way, so I focused on her unique name and her number, which is seventeen. Her poem uses her name plus sixteen verbs to show what she can do.

The toughest to write about were the scorers. They are often the stars because they put points on the board, but I had to figure out a way to distinguish each of them. Carli Lloyd could score from far away, quick as a lightning bolt, while Christen Press used her dribbling and footwork to deliver short-range goals. And of course, there's Alex. Alex Morgan was the most difficult because she made scoring look so easy. But when I realized how easy she made it look, it was easy for me to call her Automatic.

Last but not least were the goalkeepers. Briana Scurry played a big role in anchoring the '99 World Cup team to victory and also earned two Olympic gold medals, while Alyssa Naeher has anchored recent teams to two World Cup titles.

After learning more about the game and watching the women do their thing, I no longer thought of them as women players. To me, they were just ballers balling out. This book is a celebration of them.

Charles R. Smith Jr.

Dedicated to all athletes everywhere
who just want to ball out

Photo Credits
p. 3: copyright © 2015 by AP/Sydney Low
pp. 4–5: copyright © 2017 by AP/Chris Williams
p. 6: copyright © 2007 by AP/Eugene Hoshiko
p. 7: copyright © 2019 by AP/Francois Mori
pp. 8–9: copyright © 2016 by AP/Tony Gutierrez
p. 11: copyright © 2021 by AP/Mingo Nesmith/Icon Sportswire
p. 12: copyright © 2019 by Sipa USA via AP/Liu Jialiang
pp. 14–15: copyright © 2020 by AP/Trask Smith
pp. 16–17: copyright © 2017 by AP/Tony Gutierrez
pp. 18–19: copyright © 2021 by AP/Robin Alam/Icon Sportswire
pp. 20–21: copyright © 2021 by Sipa USA via AP/Sports Press Photo
pp. 22–23: copyright © 2020 by AP/Dean Mouhtaropoulos
pp. 24–25: copyright © 2011 by AP/John Biever
pp. 28–29: copyright © 1999 by Roberto Schmidt/AFP via Getty Images

First edition 2023

Library of Congress Catalog Card Number 2022908708
ISBN 978-1-5362-2533-4

23 24 25 26 27 28 CCP 10 9 8 7 6 5 4 3 2 1

Printed in Shenzhen, Guangdong, China

This book was typeset in Montserrat.
Digital artwork and typography by Lauren Pettapiece.

Candlewick Press
99 Dover Street
Somerville, Massachusetts 02144

www.candlewick.com